Jack, Benji and Rocco

First Edition
Published by Steve Marsh

Paperback ISBN 978-1-7638805-5-9
eBook ISBN 978-1-7638805-3-5

For permissions, inquiries, or additional resources, contact: contact@stemarsh.com

On our journey people will come in and out of our lives, some will be with us for the whole journey, whilst others will come and go. This is a story about 3 life long friends at different stages of their journey. They share a deep bond which allows them to consider life's ups and downs. They do so together, through trust and love in each other.

Jack, a loyal black dog who is always there for those around him. Always nearby for support.

Benji, a light coloured dog who is a fun loving ball of energy, bringing life to every moment and everyone he sees.

Rocco, a young black cat who is fearless, stands his ground but shows love and kindness to those around him.

All 3 guide each other as they walk their journey.

Why does the wind blow, asked Benji?

It reminds us that things are always moving, said Jack, we just need to embrace the flow, otherwise we may get stuck.

I don't want to get stuck, said Benji. No one does, said Jack, but sometimes we do. Remember that the wind can take us to great places, you just need to let go.

Can we go together? Asked Rocco

We'll be there to support you but sometimes we need to walk on our own, said Jack.

What if I'm scared?

Being afraid is part of life, it doesn't mean bad things will happen, it just means that we care about the outcome and it's important to us.

Will you always be with us Jack? Asked Benji

No, but that's part of life. Others will be with us on our journey but then they will leave.

We just need to value our time together and show others that we love them.

I'll miss you when you are gone, you've always been there as my friend, said Benji.

You've been my friend too, said Jack, but others will be there to support you and you will be there to support them.

Remember you are strong and those around you love you.

I like the sound of nature, it makes me realise that we aren't alone, said Rocco. It's like the music of the world that connects us all together.

I think in some way we're all connected, said Benji. From the smallest to the biggest we should look after each other.

Even the smallest can make a huge difference, said Benji, we all have our own purpose in life. We just need to find it.

And when we find it, we should hold onto it.

When I'm feeling sad I sometimes feel lost, said Rocco

We can all feel sad, said Jack. It's part of life but find the fun in life and you won't feel lost.

I love to have fun, said Benji.

We know and we love you all the more for it, said Jack. You bring a smile to all those around you. It's your gift to the world.

We each have a gift to give the world.

We do? Asked Rocco

Yes, each one of us is unique and we bring our own gifts to the world. Don't forget we are all special. You are special.

What's my gift? Asked Rocco

You are bold and fearless, said Jack. The world needs those that are brave to show the way when the dark clouds come.

What happens when the dark clouds come? Asked Benji.

You decide, said Jack. Sometimes it will feel too much and you'll want to hide away.

What do I do then? Asked Benji

You must stand tall and take one step at a time. Others will support you, but it's you who decides your own path.

Even one small step is a step in the right direction, just keep moving forwards.

Some days it will feel hard but keep moving.

When you get to the other side the sun will be shining.

You will see that the hard times allowed you to learn, grow and become who you are today.

Sometimes I have lots of thoughts running through my head, said Rocco, and I don't know what to do.

Just breathe, said Jack, and let the thoughts settle.

Make the choice simple and your heart will let you know how to move forwards.

Your heart always knows the way forward, just remember to listen to it.

Sometimes others can upset me, said Rocco, and I can get angry and sad all at the same time.

Don't let the negative words of others affect your enjoyment of life.

Live life how you want to and follow your dreams.

We should also try to understand those that hurt us, said Benji.

Through kindness and love we can learn to forgive.

Others may be hurting too. Without forgiveness there is only pain.

I'm tired from all this walking, said Jack. My legs aren't as young as they used to be.

We'll support you, said Benji, you've supported us throughout the years. It's now our turn to help you.

Thank you, dear friends.

Sometimes we can forget to ask for help, as it feels hard, said Benji.

Those that truly love us will always be there to help and support us.

What happens if I fail, said Rocco.

You will fail, replied Jack, and that's how it should be. We learn from our mistakes and they allow us to grow.

Nothing in life is perfect.

I wish we could stop time, said Benji.

If time didn't keep moving then we wouldn't value how important it is, replied Rocco.

Remember time is precious, we can't get it back, said Jack.

Spend it with those who make you smile and love you for who you are.

Don't relive the past or worry about the future. Be present and enjoy the moment, it's the only point in time you can control.

I love spending time with others, said Benji. I could do it all day.

Sometimes I just like spending time on my own, said Rocco. I like the quiet.

I like being nearby others, but in my own space added Jack.

I think we should respect how others want to spend their time, said Benji.

Very wise, replied Jack, if you like your own space it doesn't mean you don't care.

We are all different and spend time in our own way, we should respect that.

Without friends I think I would be sad, said Rocco.

Finding friends is important, I'm glad I found you two, said Benji.

It's important to find friends who treat you with respect, love and for who you are.

If someone is having a bad day, a simple hello from those who care can make all the difference and make their day shine again.

You make everyday shine for us, replied Jack and Rocco.

There is a river ahead, how do we get across? Asked Benji.

With patience and belief we can overcome any challenge, said Rocco. I'll show you.

Your boldness inspires us every day. We need those in our life who inspire us to take up the next leap, said Jack.

It can sometimes feel hard but we need to believe. You help me believe.

Instead of asking 'why' we should do something, we should ask 'why not', said Jack. It opens up lots of doors in our life, to greater experiences and connections.

Just try it and see where it takes you.

You make me feel safe Jack, said Rocco.

Those in our life who make us feel safe, make us feel like we're home, it feels warm and we feel loved.

I always feel at home with you, said Benji

As we walk through life we'll all have ups and downs on the way, but on the journey we'll hopefully have people in our lives that guide us and lift us up. Choose those in your life that believe in you and make you smile.

You'll make mistakes on the way, and others will make mistakes too, but that's part of life, it's how we respond to those mistakes and how we learn from them. Forgive yourself and forgive others.

Life is there to live, take the chances and be bold, but also to quietly reflect. People come into our lives for a reason, even if we don't know why. Embrace those who are important to you and love them with all your heart.

Hopefully these 3 friends have shown you the way.

About the Author

Steve Marsh is a writer, photographer, and accidental philosopher whose work blends dry wit with quiet observation. Born in Wigan, a working-class town in the north of England, Steve grew up with a healthy dose of northern humour and a knack for finding meaning in the mundane. In his twenties, he packed his bags and moved to Australia in search of something more, sunshine, freedom, perspective...and maybe a slightly slower pace of life.

That leap became a turning point. Surrounded by Australia's wide open spaces and salt-soaked coastlines, Steve found the space to reflect, create, and explore what it means to live a life that's both thoughtful and lighthearted. Whether behind the lens or in front of the keyboard, his work encourages people to pause, notice the small things, and approach life with curiosity, humour, and a bit more care.

Steve's work is a refreshingly honest and often funny take on navigating the chaos of modern living with a little less stress and a little more perspective. Through a mix of humour, reflection, and everyday insight, he encourages *readers to slow down, laugh at themselves, and maybe, even just a little, rethink how they show up in the world.*

When he's not writing or shooting photographs, you'll find him exploring the Australian coastline, indulging in long walks and runs, tinkering with technology or answering an endless stream of wonderfully weird questions from his kids.

Discover more at stemarsh.com

www.ingramcontent.com/pod-product-compliance
Lightning Source LLC
LaVergne TN
LVHW050611100826
845148LV00015B/3226
9781763880559